FALL 2019
IN THIS ISSUE:

THE NEW KIND OF HUDSON VALLEY REALTY
| P.3

A HISTORIC HUDSON VALLEY FARMHOUSE REINVENTED BY DUNCAN AVENUE DESIGN STUDIO
| P.6

BRANDING HUDSON VALLEY REAL ESTATE FOR THE GLOBAL MARKET
| P.20

ESCAPE NYC LIFE IN THIS TRANQUIL RETREAT CREATED BY HUDSON DESIGN
| P.47

#FARMHOUSEREINVENTED

| FROM THE EDITORS:

Alexander Maxwell Realty is gaining ground by the hour while we are taking our design and marketing business to a whole new level. There are a few things coming up that we can't talk about yet, but hang on, the next big thing is almost here!

In the meantime we are excited to feature HUDSON DESIGN and Jennifer Lynn in this issue and are thankful for the opportunity to feature Hudson Valley's best design work.

Maxwell & Dino Alexander

© 2019 Hudson Valley Style Magazine
A Duncan Avenue Group Publication
Contact Us:
World/US: 1-845-518-2750
HudsonValley.Style

HUDSON VALLEY **STYLE** 1

ALEXANDER MAXWELL REALTY | UPGRADE YOUR REALTY™
MEET THE NEW KIND OF REALTY

DINO ALEXANDER
Principal Broker, Alexander Maxwell Realty

New York State Licensed Real Estate Broker and Chief Executive Officer at the Duncan Avenue Group, Dino is an Expert in Business and Economics and has a vast experience in real estate, high-end fashion, and retail industries. Dino believes that Hudson Valley has a unique role in the Global Economy and the Modern Rustic Hudson Valley Style represents It on a Global scale.

Alexander Maxwell Realty is not just a Team of Realtors, but also a family. We know that a happy family starts with a happy home. We love to help our clients to find a happy place while investing in their future.

MAXWELL ALEXANDER
N.Y.S. Licensed Real Estate Sales Person, Alexander Maxwell Realty

Designer, Creative Director, Editor-in-Chief of the Hudson Valley Style Magazine, and World Class Brand Strategist, Maxwell has elevated creative-, design- and cultural value for hundreds of brands all around the World, ranging from technology startups, wellness & fitness brands, to Fortune 500 companies and globally renown non-profit organizations and government agencies.

As a Licensed Real Estate Salesperson, experienced Real Estate Investor/Developer, and Chief Design Officer of the Duncan Avenue Group, Maxwell represents Authentic Hudson Valley™ properties designed by the Award-Winning Duncan Avenue Design Studio.

WHY LIST WITH @ALMAXREALTY?

When you choose Alexander Maxwell Realty you choose a company which helps to invest in your future, to us you are not a one-off client – we form long-standing relationships with all our valued customers. To us, your property is a work of art and it is exactly how our All-inclusive Strategic Marketing Package will present it to the World:

1. LET'S MEET AND BRAINSTORM

At our first meeting and walkthrough of your property, we will discuss the initial market assessment, pricing, and marketing strategy. We will talk about your goals and the best way to reach them. We'll help you to achieve an optimal market positioning based on your goals, whether it is the sale price or timing.

ALEXANDER MAXWELL REALTY | UPGRADE YOUR REALITY™
MEET THE NEW KIND OF REALTY

2. IT'S TIME FOR A FACELIFT

Whether it is a brand new construction or a 200-year-old castle, your property will get a facelift based on the Strategy we agreed upon at the first step. It could be as little as a few expert staging recommendations or even more extensive measures such as paint or landscape improvement. We'll show you the numbers and how a small tweak at the initial stage can deliver tremendous return at the closing. Our industry partners can get the job done timely and efficiently, we even provide easy financing options if necessary.

3. PR AND MARKETING GEARS ARE STARTING TO SPIN

Next, we will start executing the Strategy: whether it is an award-winning real estate photography, property branding, aerial/drone imaging, video walkthrough, social media campaign, search engines optimization, feature in a critically acclaimed publication with a global reach, or all of the above - it is all included in our Strategic Marketing Package at no additional cost to you!

4. HERE IS THE FUN PART!

When the listing is ready to be presented in all of its glory, we will hold the first open house event and invite potential buyers, real estate brokers, industry leaders, news outlets and members of the public. At the end of the event, we will distribute a press-release, interviews, and event photos through 250+ media/pr/news channels and push the property listing via MLS, Zillow, Realtor.com, Trulia and 100+ other real estate marketing platforms.

5. BUILDING WINDMILLS, NOT WALLS

Real Estate is a dynamic and ever-changing market. Those who can harness the energy of the winds of change will eventually win. During the time on the market, we will help you to negotiate offers and adjust your Strategy based on the market feedback.

6. PAPER-PUSHING IS STILL A THING, EVEN WHEN IT'S DIGITAL

Selling Real Estate is a process that involves many team players and an enormous workflow of documents. Our team will assist you and your legal team with paperwork all the way from the beginning until closing and we will stay on top of the timeline, making sure everything is on track!

STYLE, DESIGN, AND INTELLIGENCE SPEAK VOLUMES. WE FLY WITH EAGLES, SO SHOULD YOUR REAL ESTATE MARKETING CAMPAIGN. TAKE IT TO THE NEXT LEVEL WITH @ALMAXREALTY

#FARMHOUSEREINVENTED
[MARLBORO, NY]

A HISTORIC HUDSON VALLEY FARMHOUSE REINVENTED

STORY & PHOTOGRAPHY BY **MAXWELL ALEXANDER**

Welcome to the historic (circa 1870) Hudson Valley Farmhouse in the heart of legendary Marlboro, NY. It has been completely reimagined by the Award-Winning Duncan Avenue Design Studio and has become an inspiring, stylish and extremely comfortable zero-emissions 21st century smart home just minutes away from NYC. Situated on top of a hill and an acre of picturesque landscape, it could become your turnkey second-home, a vacation home, rental or investment property, or an authentic Hudson Valley Style dream home for generations to come.

The Farmhouse has been renovated with style, design, sustainability, functionality, and comfort in mind and incorporates more than a dozen smart technology, energy efficiency, and sustainability features.

Contemporary open concept floorplan, glass french doors and 210° wraparound porch with 3-season outdoor dining space blur the line between indoor and outdoor living and allow residents and guests to enjoy a true connection with surrounding nature.

Wake up to the sunrise shining through double glass doors on the east side of the house and watch the warm sunset rays shining through plenty of energy-efficient windows and french doors on the west. High-end finishes such as sustainable bamboo hardwood floors, sustainable concrete countertops, solid wood kitchen cabinets with soft closing drawers, energy star stainless steel appliances, and designer light fixtures are only a few of the updates along with a brand-new central HVAC heat pump system controlled by smart Nest thermostat with two-zone sensors.

CONTEMPORARY
SMART
FLOOR PLAN

Brand new roof, utilities, and all LED lighting bring additional value and comfort for many years to come. The property features a beautiful designer pergola on the edge of the hill with an opportunity for the in-ground infinity pool. Property's sun number is 91 and is all set for installation of your own solar farm that will take the property go 100% off-grid.

#FARMHOUSEREINVENTED

[MARLBORO, NY]

THIS SPECTACULAR KITCHEN IS READY TO HOST YOUR YOUTUBE COOKING SHOW

The kitchen is the heart of any home and this modern rustic kitchen is a perfect playground for a seasoned cook or an aspiring YouTube cooking show host. It's not just the size of the kitchen, but also the contemporary and eco-conscious features that are also impressive.

← Copper Tile

SUSTAINABLE CONCRETE & WOOD COUNTERTOPS

This kitchen has a lot of character thanks to the sophisticated/industrial look of concrete countertops. They are not just trendy, but also environmentally-friendly. One of the unique characteristics of concrete is that this material will evolve and adopt character over time, so the appearance of your counters will improve with age. Concrete counters are durable and heat-resistant for all of you avid bakers out there. The material is non-toxic, does not emit VOCs unlike plastics/polymers and is a sustainable material, unlike granite or marble. Concrete is a friend of the environment in all stages of its life span, from raw material production to demolition, making it a natural choice for sustainable home construction.

STAINLESS STEEL ENERGY STAR APPLIANCES

Stainless Steel Energy Star Appliances are an important accord in an overall symphony of this amazing and functional kitchen. They are positioned in the most efficient way to ensure an easy cooking process. The kitchen features range hood vented outside of the house and stylish yet environmentally-friendly electric range. Hudson Valley region energy providers offer an option to switch to 100% renewable electricity from wind and solar, so the electric range makes a lot of sense.

#FARMHOUSEREINVENTED
[MARLBORO, NY]

NATURAL PATTERNS CERAMIC TILE MATTE BLACK ACCENTS

Natural look and natural materials. This time we went with darker accents colors, but overall both bathrooms in this house are bright and airy.

FLOATING VANITIES & BARN DOORS, CERAMIC TILE, DESIGNER LED LIGHT FIXTURES, AN ABUNDANCE OF LIGHT & SPACE CREATE AN INSPIRING SPA-LIKE EXPERIENCE

HIGH-END MODERN RUSTIC BATHROOMS

#FARMHOUSEREINVENTED
[MARLBORO, NY]

Overlooking beautiful Hudson Valley skyline with plenty of windows on every side of the home it feels open, bright and spacious. The wrap-around porch is signature farmhouse curb appeal feature and welcomes and inspires you just upon entering the home. Via double glass french doors outdoor space seamlessly flows into an open concept kitchen and living area ready for family gatherings, entertainment, and inspiring everyday living.

BRANDING HUDSON VALLEY REAL ESTATE FOR THE GLOBAL MARKET

BY DINO ALEXANDER (PRINCIPAL BROKER, ALEXANDER MAXWELL REALTY)

In today's market, real estate investors, as well as regular buyers are spoilt for choice. Even the best location is no longer enough when it comes to competing on a Global Market and this is when Strategic Branding comes into play. Luxury Real Estate Properties do not sell overnight and require a long-term Brand Strategy.

By definition, brand strategy is a long-term plan for the development of a successful brand in order to achieve specific goals. A well-defined and executed brand strategy affects all aspects of a business and is directly connected to consumer needs, emotions, and competitive environments. In real estate stakes are much higher just because the subject of the branding process is a single product and the goal is one transaction - property sale.

A WELL-DEFINED AND EXECUTED BRAND STRATEGY AFFECTS ALL ASPECTS OF A BUSINESS & IS DIRECTLY CONNECTED TO CONSUMER NEEDS, EMOTIONS, & COMPETITIVE ENVIRONMENTS

Alexander Maxwell Realty has partnered with award-winning Duncan Avenue Studio and together has more than a decade of experience branding products and services competing on the Global Market. Our clients include world-renown global economy players, Fortune 500 Companies, technology startups, wellness, and fitness brands, medical, manufacturing, real estate brands, NGOs as well as government agencies. Each property listed with Alexander Maxwell Realty becomes a unique World-Class Brand and presented to the local and global audience of real estate buyers through our high-end PR and marketing channels.

Logon to almaxrealty.com to schedule your listing consultation.

SARAGOLDEN.COM

[KITCHEN DESIGN TRENDS]

DESIGN YOUR KITCHEN LIKE A MILLENNIAL

by **Maxwell Alexander**

[KITCHEN DESIGN TRENDS]

Ah, Millennials, it warms my heart writing about Us – the most consciously awaken generation humans produced so far. We literally design the world around us in sync with Nature and the Universe. So what does it means to design a kitchen like a Millennial?

KITCHEN IS THE NEW LIVING ROOM

Millennials are awakening to the wisdom of the Cosmic Intelligence and taking into account the experience of the previous generations, they realize that anything related to food is crucial to our existence, not only because of the physical nourishment and wellbeing but also as a spiritual connection with our innate nature and other human beings. Sitting around a fire pit while preparing and sharing food, socializing, creating stories and memories is where life happened for our ancestors who were a lot closely connected to Nature. Millennials spend a great deal of their time not only socializing, but also working in coffee shops recreating the ancient environment and conditions where humans operate most efficiently while feeling their best. Now that Millennials are finally ready to build their own nests, and knowing that they will spend most of their time with the family cooking organic meals and socializing in the fully equipped kitchen, they bring the coffee shop concept with them. Walls are crumbling, dining rooms are being torn down – Millenials are hard at work making the open floor plan a reality.

Whew! The era of plastics is officially over! Thank you, but no thank you, Babyboomers! We are back to basics and embracing wood, steel, concrete, and natural stone. Walls, floors, furniture, and appliances are things we touch and in the air, we breathe, so why should it emit toxic fumes in the space where we spend most of our time? Plus, the use of sustainable materials like wood proactively protects the climate and serves as a repository of carbon emissions. Millennials are ditching their mom's plastic countertops and replacing them with simple, environmentally-friendly and cost-efficient concrete or quartz counters.

Millennial way or not, it's a great time to rethink your kitchen design. **Duncan Avenue Design Studio** is Hudson Valley's leading interior design agency and in collaboration with **Tough Construct | Hudson Valley**, they can execute a jaw-dropping overhaul of your kitchen space.

Visit ToughConstruct.com to learn more.

What you won't find in the Millennial's kitchen/living/dining space is a TV. Fortunately, Millennials hadn't had a chance to get hooked on the whole "cable" idea, whatever entertainment they need to get is at everyone's fingertips, so there is no reason to cover all the beautiful natural concrete/stucco walls with obnoxious plastic panels. In the meantime, a chalkboard is a great alternative to digital overload, so why not make an entire wall as a billboard for family-wide announcements, recipe display or a point of creative collaboration!

MILLENNIALS ARE BACK TO BASICS WHEN IT COMES TO CHOOSING INTERIOR MATERIALS

[KITCHEN DESIGN TRENDS]

INDUSTRIAL AUTHENTIC RUSTIC

CLASSY INDUSTRIAL LOOK, MODERN RUSTIC STYLE

Modern Rustic, Industrial Style is hot, especially with Millennials who appreciate reusing and recycling while staying classy and sophisticated. If you squint your eyes in Millennial's kitchen, you'll see a lot of grey-ish, brown-ish, black-ish and whitish colors reflecting in natural light. Remember the caves we lived in generations ago? I bet you'd see the same picture if you squint your eyes in one of those. Industrial shelving solutions are so in and you still got a chance to find a great deal at a nearby scrap metal place or a flea market. Hit garage sales this weekend for unique and environmentally conscious furniture. Dig into your grandma's attic for one of a kind decor for your Millennials-inspired kitchen.

FENG SHUI, YING YANG, BALANCE...

Wellness is about balance and Millennials take both very seriously. Whether you are a fan of centuries-old feng shui traditions, understand why Ying can't survive without Yang, or just following a common sense and balanced approach, you'd know that too much of good could be just as bad. Balance is the key, especially in kitchen design. Space should flow naturally, with enough square footage to breathe. Entrance to the kitchen should be either wide or cleared of any obstructions. Having storage in the kitchen is essential, however, try to hide unappealing items in cabinets below eye level and balance shelving with clear wall space ("white space" in layout design). If you use feng shui practice to decorate your home, you know the power of plants. Plants attract good energy. They also absorb negative energy and distractions. Surround yourself, neatly, with large smooth-leaved plants in earthenware pots. The plants and pottery represent the mountains and create supportive energy. Two good plant choices are the golden pothos and areca palm.

SCIENTIFICALLY JUSTIFIED & CULTURALLY EMBRACED SMART LIGHTING DESIGN

Lighting is a crucial element in interior design and if you are spending most of your time in your kitchen/living/dining/socializing space, you should know the facts. Lighting is like a lens that reveals the reality around us, and if the lens has an incorrect prescription, it will sure to give you a headache and affect your health negatively. Millennials are the smartest generation in the history of human civilization, they dictate the new lighting design trends:

An abundance of natural light is the best way to go. Our bodies are designed to thrive in the natural light, so it's important to welcome it inside the kitchen space.
LED Edison bulbs use a lot less energy and generate warmer light frequencies that create a cozy and stress-free ambiance.
Oversized industrial light fixtures are trendy and great at preventing the artificial light sources shine directly into your eyes and guide the light rays where they are needed.

WHO IS YOUR BUYER?

[MILLENNIALS]

 **36%**
[THE LARGEST MARKET SHARE]

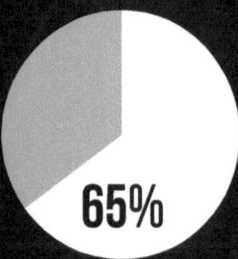 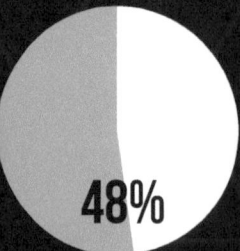 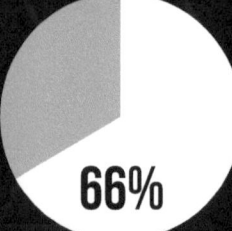 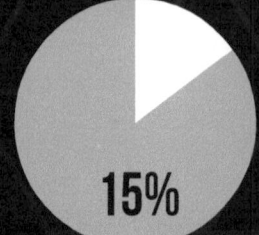

65% — FIRST-TIME HOME BUYERS
48% — HAVE CHILDREN
66% — MARRIED COUPLES
15% — UNMARRIED COUPLES

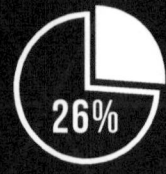 **26%** [OF ALL HOMEBUYERS] **GENERATION X** 38-52 Y/O

$104,700 [MEDIAN INCOME]

MOST LIKELY TO BE MARRIED & MOST LIKELY TO HAVE CHILDREN

[MOST RACIALLY & ETHNICALLY DIVERSE]
26% IDENTIFYING THEY ARE A RACE OTHER THAN WHITE/CAUCASIAN

BUY THE LARGEST HOMES IN MEDIAN SQFT.
PURCHASE THE HIGHEST MEDIAN PRICED HOMES

[YOUNGER BABY BOOMERS] 53-62 Y/O
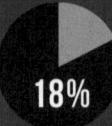 **18%**

[OLDER BABY BOOMERS] 63-71 Y/O
14%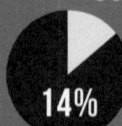

[THE SILENT GENERATION] 72-92 Y/O
6%

28 HUDSON VALLEY STYLE

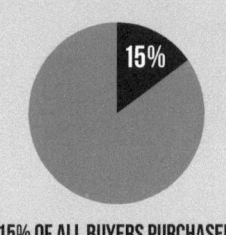

15% OF ALL BUYERS PURCHASED NEW CONSTRUCTION

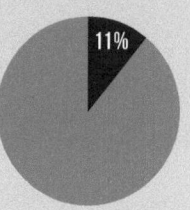

11% OF MILLENNIALS PURCHASED NEW CONSTRUCTION

85% PURCHASED PREVIOUSLY OWNED HOMES
[MILLENNIALS: 89%]

MOST IMPORTANT ENVIRONMENTAL FEATURES:
HEATING & COOLING COSTS

TYPICAL HOME RECENTLY PURCHASED
1,870 SQFT.
3 BDRM.
2 BATH.

90%

"90% OF BUYERS UNDER AGE OF 62 CONSIDER PHOTOGRAPHY AS THE MOST IMPORTANT FEATURE WHEN SEARCHING ONLINE"

DATA SOURCE: 2018 HOME BUYER AND SELLER GENERATIONAL TRENDS REPORT BY THE NATIONAL ASSOCIATION OF REALTORS®

SELLING YOUR PROPERTY?
ASK US ABOUT **COMPLIMENTARY** ALL-INCLUSIVE STRATEGIC MARKETING PACKAGE

LOG ON TO ALMAXREALTY.COM & JOIN US ON INSTAGRAM! @ALMAXREALTY

[PRESENTED BY ALMAXREALTY.COM]

[HUDSON VALLEY STYLE TREND]

2019 INTERIOR DESIGN TREND: BARN DOORS

Barn doors are no longer an outdoor feature, but a stylish yet rustic Hudson Valley Style interior design trend. Known for their functionality and space-saving features, they are in high demand among ToughConstruct clients in Hudson Valley's Cornwall on Hudson, New Windsor, Newburgh, Wallkill, Goshen, Pine Bush, and Beacon areas. With the help of ToughConstruct (2018 Hudson Valley Style, Design & Sustainability Awards Winner), discover why adding a barn door is an ideal home improvement project that will bring modern rustic style into your home.

BARN DOORS ARE A PERFECT ELEMENT TO CONNECT ROOMS WITHIN AN OPEN FLOORPLAN

BARN DOORS ARE A PERFECT CONVERSATION PIECE

Interior doors are not just art hanging on the wall, but also serves an important function, they also can showcase a homeowner's style and personality. Barn

CUSTOM BARN DOORS ARE TRENDY YET CLASSY

Just like a piece of clothing, home decor often goes out of style, however, barn doors have been around for centuries and are an essential part of the Authentic Hudson Valley Style. Many Hudson Valley homeowners go with a modern, sophisticated look, rustic wood look or with a chalkboard barn door that adds another layer of functionality in the kitchen or a kid's room.

Adding a custom-built barn door in your Hudson Valley home could dramatically

As open floor plans gain popularity among homeowners in the greater Hudson Valley region, interior doors are evolving as well. Barn doors are one of the most efficient yet trendy approaches to connect adjacent rooms into one open floorplan space.

"The organic modern rustic look of custom barn doors adds warmth and cosy feeling into an interior," says Designer Maxwell Alexander of Duncan Avenue Design Studio. "The space-saving flexibility of a barn door is an important function of adjusting and controlling interior environment to one's liking." Conventional hinge-mounted doors are out of fashion and take 2 times more space than a barn door that slides on a rolling track.

doors are a perfect conversation piece when entertaining family and friends. If your home is lacking a statement piece that inspires creativity and sparks conversation, contact ToughConstruct today to get a free quote for a custom-built barn door that will perfectly fit your space. Take a look at brand door examples of ToughConstruct's previous clients.

improve interior design of a space, not only from a visual perspective but also from a functional perspective. Imagine adding a few more square feet of space that doesn't have to overlap with a door rotating on hinges? High-quality, custom-built brand doors by Hudson Valley's best contractor will refresh your interiors and make you ready to meet one of the most beautiful seasons in the Hudson Valley!

MODERN FARMHOUSE IN WOODSTOCK, NY

INTERIOR DESIGN PROJECT
BY JENNIFER LYNN

[DESIGNER JENNIFER LYNN]

[HUDSON VALLEY STYLE INTERIOR DESIGN]

Interview by **Maxwell Alexander**
Photography by **Leyla Cadabal**

Just last week I've had an opportunity to sit down with Designer Jennifer Lynn, the Owner, and President of Jennifer Lynn Interiors. I've been watching her work on social media for a while now and was eager to get to know what inspires her amazingly inviting and beautifully classic interiors.

"My true passion has always been interior design but arrived at this place in life down a long windy road. As an educator for 17 years, in the Hudson Valley, making a career change was insurmountable. Call it a "mid-life" crisis if you wish, but it has been the best decision of my career life! Designing for others these last four years brings joy, excitement, and beauty to the Hudson Valley."- said Jennifer when I asked her what brought her to the Hudson Valley and how she got into the interior design business.

When I first saw Leyla's photographs of the Woodstock House, I was very intrigued, because I knew it's an older architecture yet space looked very open and contemporary. "The house itself belongs to a lovely family who had dreams of transforming it into their second home and a part-time vacation rental."- said Jennifer, "Before renovations, the 1950s had several small, closed-off spaces. Our goal was to make it a more open concept floor plan. The space needed to support lots of families, guests, and good times."- she added.

"So who saw the potential and why?" - I asked.

Jennifer: "Prior to the demo, the clients, contractor and I toured the property discussed ideas and then began to draw up the plans. Collaboratively, the clients and JLI worked together to create a plan that was perfect for their new home. JLI proposed to remove walls in the plan and started to plan out the built-ins in the foyer and living room. We sketched out 3 options for the kitchen area. The client settled on the final layout. By opening up this first floor, we saw the potential for the home to host large parties and guest when rented out for a week. It is perfectly located in Woodstock NY for skiers, leaf peepers and those looking for a mountain retreat.

On demo week, we removed one wall between the kitchen and dining room and another between the dining room and living room. This opened up the first floor immensely. Upstairs, the rooms stayed intact. In the master bedroom, we expanded the bathroom to make it more functional as well as aesthetically beautiful. This vision was seen by the contracting team and we were 100% on board."

Maxwell Alexander: "What was the main goal for the renovation and what was behind the new layout, style, finishes?"

Jennifer Lynn:
"After our initial consultation with the clients, we set these goals together:

Create an open concept space for family time and entertaining
Incorporate several additional sleeping options for children and guests
Tailor the design to a clean, modern farmhouse look
Layer in some fun color!
Using visual communication, the client was very excited about a modern farmhouse aesthetic. They loved clean, crisp lines and wow moments of color throughout. As for finishes, we have focused on black matte throughout a majority of the design in the

home. To keep things fun, we add splashes gold accents in the kitchen hardware, and master bedroom lighting and hardware. The tile selections in the bathrooms were timeless. They will quickly bring a return on their investment as they will sustain effortlessly over time. We used marble selections mixed with ceramic tile as a way to keep costs down. As for the flooring throughout the home, we used 100% oak wood floors and stained a medium brown to keep the space feeling warm. In the kitchen, we used marble tiles on the backsplash and LG Sigma quartz countertops. We also used LG clarino in both bathrooms to bring in additional warmth."

I also noticed that in addition to sophisticated and authentic Hudson Valley Style aesthetics, the property now also features sustainability improvements, such as energy-efficient lighting, energy star appliances, and smart climate control. "In a time where your design choices impact the world around us, it is important to make selections accordingly. We have a social responsibility to provide a universal design that has a focus on safety and security as well as longevity and sustainability."- added Jennifer.

[HUDSON VALLEY STYLE INTERIOR DESIGN]

REAL ESTATE PHOTOGRAPHY 101

61% MORE VIEWS ONLINE WITH PROFESSIONAL PHOTOS

UP TO 47% HIGHER ASKING PRICE/SQFT

80% OF BUYERS
CITED THEY WOULDN'T EVEN CONSIDER A LISTING WITHOUT PHOTOGRAPHS

98% OF BUYERS
THINK PROFESSIONAL PHOTOS ARE MOST USEFUL WHEN LOOKING FOR HOME ONLINE

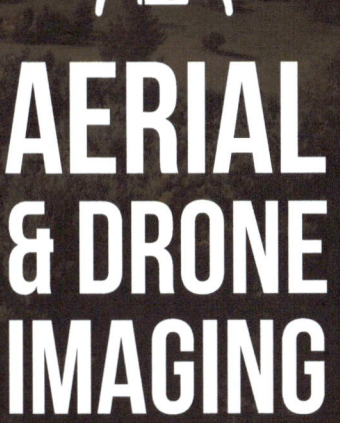

AERIAL & DRONE IMAGING

CONSIDER THESE HIGH-TECH UPGRADES

DUNCANAVENUE™
HUDSON VALLEY REAL ESTATE SERVICES

SCHEDULE YOUR PHOTOSHOOT @
DUNCANAVENUE.COM

STATISTICS SOURCE:
NATIONAL ASSOCIATION OF REALTORS

PROFESSIONAL LIGHTING

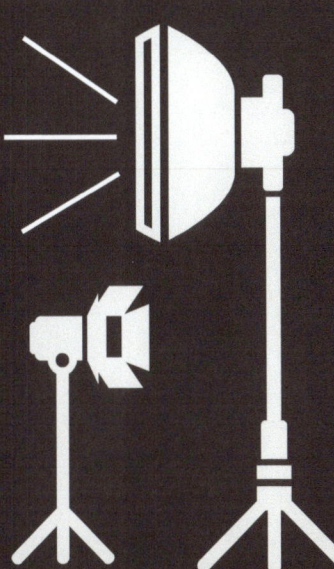

DSLR CAMERAS & LENSES

PROFESSIONAL RETOUCHING

+ DIGITAL STAGING

[HUDSON VALLEY STYLE LIVING]

[O'CONNELL'S SUMMER RESIDENCE]

*Photo Story and Interview by **Maxwell Alexander***

Myles and Desiree O'Connell

Brooklynites Myles and Desire O'Connell were frequent visitors to the Catskills and the Hudson Valley, up until they bumped into each other on a hike near Woodstock. Soon after, Myles proposed to Desire on the top of the Panther Mountain in Shandaken. It was a matter of time for them to start thinking about putting their roots down (even just for the Summer season as it usually goes.)

"Of all of the fantastic small towns in the Catskills, we fell in love with Woodstock. Every time we went on a hike, we always drove through the village to shop the windows and have a late lunch before driving home." - explained Myles. "When the property became available, I think we both jumped on the opportunity. We loved that it was located directly in the middle of the village, walking distance to all of the boutiques, and great restaurants."

From our own experience renovating 200-year-old properties, we know that when something like this happens, it has to be a match made in heaven, and I am referring to both personal chemistry as a couple and connection with a house as well. This house got really lucky, just take a look at one of the "Before" shots. At the same time, it makes me really proud to see Millennials like Myles and Desire being able to recognize an opportunity behind those thick layers of borderline-psychedelic paint. It really does takes guts to get into something like this one!

[HUDSON VALLEY STYLE LIVING]

And yes, it worked out amazing, all in the authentic, modern yet rustic Hudson Valley Style. I knew how a 200-y/o craftsman or a gingerbread type of a home might look like on the inside, so it was almost a magical experience when I first walked in and saw the space. It felt very open, airy and yet so appropriate and somehow "this is how it should've been in the first place". Beautiful rustic beams on the ceiling, wood+brick columns, cozy and perfectly refinished hardwood floors, sophisticated furniture and decor, glass, metal, and warm+dynamic Edison lights make this home a Modern Rustic epiphany that should be on everyone's bucket list. Lucky you, the property is on Airbnb when Desire and Myles are out of town, so there is an opportunity to experience it.

"It was important to us that the kitchen was connected to both the dining and living rooms - and that both had large windows the patio. We also completely gut renovated the kitchen and added a new sink and shower to the bathroom, and decided to open up the ceiling to expose the original beams in the living room. It not only added a ton of character and warmth to the house but also it created additional space. Donna LeMoine from Atlas Home Construction did a fantastic job on the build out."

"We also completely leveled the backyard, planted trees, perennials, and seasonal flowers, as well as a new patio, walkway, and bocce court. Bill Stack from Mountain Gardens Landscaping had a real vision for the yard."

This is a great example of how ideas of environmentally responsible design could be so relevant and stylish at the same time. New construction homes, after all, are not on the trendy list of the new generation of homebuyers, and especially in the Hudson Valley, projects like this one lead the way to a more sustainable future.

DA SKY™

AERIAL PHOTOGRAPHY

by

DUNCAN**AVENUE**™

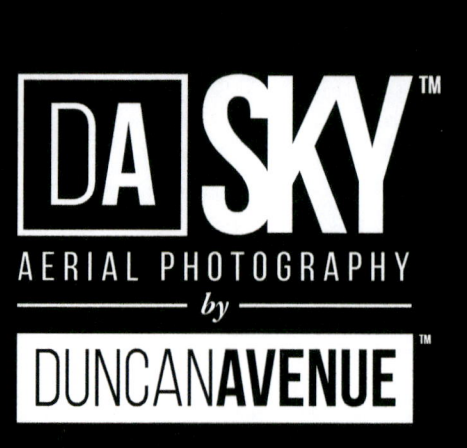

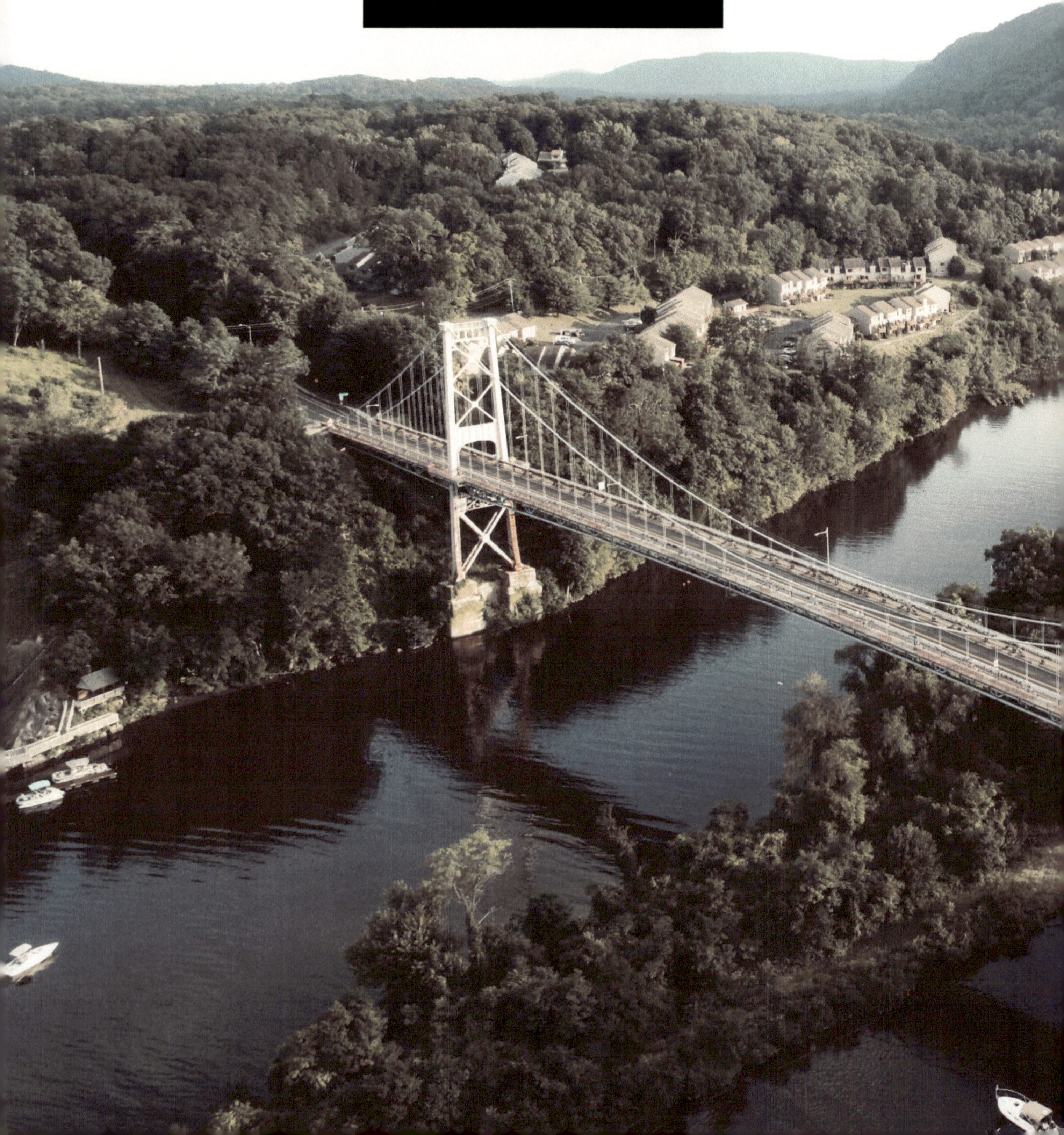

[DUNCANAVENUE.COM/SKY]

[da-aromatherapy.com]

KEEP NATURE NATURAL.

Our Natural Insect Repellents are made with Organic Essential Oils and are free of chemical pesticides that are harmful to your health and the environment.

da™ aromatherapy

FALL ESSENTIALS

NATURAL HAND SANITIZERS WITH ORGANIC ESSENTIAL OILS
by DA Aromatherapy Collection

Working out at the gym or taking a Savasana on your yoga mat? Protect yourself and loved ones plus get an aromatherapy boost on the go with these natural hand sanitizers. DA Aromatherapy Hand Sanitizing Mists with Organic Essential Oils are effective against 99.9% of common germs and bacteria.

DA-AROMATHERAPY.COM
◇◇◇◇◇◇◇◇◇◇◇◇◇◇
$9.00

WOODLAND TRAILS BLEND
by DA Aromatherapy Collection

This natural insect repellent is made with 7 organic essential oils, it provides broad-spectrum protection and repels mosquitoes and ticks, fleas and many other pesky insects. The Best Natural Tick and Mosquito Repellent Spray is created for direct skin contact, safe for Humans and Pets and featuring exclusive Woodland Trails™ blend of Organic Lemongrass, Eucalyptus Lemon, and Eucalyptus Globulus, Cedarwood (Cedar Oil), Rosemary, Clove, and Lavender Essential Oils.

Our signature Tick and Mosquito Natural Spray will keep you sting and bite-free without the use of pesticides that are harmful to humans, the environment at large and especially good insects like honeybees. Our natural tick and mosquito repellent can help to protect you when sprayed in a room, on the balcony, in a car, on the body, and even on your clothes without staining.

DA-AROMATHERAPY.COM
◇◇◇◇◇◇◇◇◇◇◇◇◇◇
$17.00

INSPIRING AROMATHERAPY MIST WITH ORGANIC LAVENDER AND SANDALWOOD ESSENTIAL OILS - WINDS OF STORMKING™
by DA Aromatherapy Collection

A luxurious and sensual fragrance of rich, woodsy sandalwood accord and beautiful flowery notes of lavender and spice. Winds of Stormking™ Essential Oil Blend perfectly captures the cool mountain breezes, sun sparkles in the Hudson River waters and lush foliage of the Hudson Valley.

DA-AROMATHERAPY.COM
◇◇◇◇◇◇◇◇◇◇◇◇◇◇
$9.00

FIND YOUR HOME

#ALMAXREALTY
#HUDSONVALLEY
#REALESTATE

ALEXANDER MAXWELL REALTY | EQUAL HOUSING OPPORTUNITY

ALMAXREALTY.COM // 845-518-2750
309 WALL ST, SUITE 1, KINGSTON, NY 12401
N.Y.S. LIC.# 10491207973

[HUDSON VALLEY STYLE ARCHITECTURE]

ESCAPE NEW YORK CITY LIFE IN THIS TRANQUIL HUDSON VALLEY STYLE RETREAT CREATED BY HUDSON DESIGN

Lake House Project by HUDSON DESIGN
Interior Design by Jarlath Mellett
Photography Courtesy of HUDSON DESIGN

Hudson Valley is home to many world-renown architectural & design marvels and architecture firm HUDSON DESIGN is keeping up with the tradition of creating structures that merge art and architecture with aesthetic acumen. They just unveiled their latest project in Putnam Valley: a modern, minimalist home designed for a picturesque lakefront setting on Lake Oscawana.

In line with authentic Hudson Valley Style, the home is designed in sync with nature and on the inside features open floor plans and floor-to-ceiling structural steel windows that create unobstructed panoramic views of the surrounding landscape.

"CARE WAS GIVEN TO MINIMIZE THE DETAILS, SO THE OBSERVER WOULD BE LESS AWARE OF THE HOME'S ENCLOSURE AND MORE AWARE OF THEIR EXPERIENCE SURROUNDED BY LUSH WOODLANDS. WHAT DETAILS WE DID WANT TO FEATURE, WE CHOSE TO DO SO WITH CRAFTSMANSHIP AND AUTHENTIC MATERIALS," SAYS JAMES COPELAND, FOUNDER, HUDSON DESIGN.

A cantilevered deck, Garapa hardwood decking and ceiling finish, custom acrylic finish on the fireplace and low-maintenance and fade resistant Englert aluminum panels are just a few design highlights of this 3,000 square-foot home. Use of concrete, wood, steel, and glass as primary building materials proves Hudson Design's commitment to Sustainable Design practices that are not only good for the wellbeing of the home's residents but better for the environment at large. It also boasts a stormwater management system, which prevents direct runoff into the lake, among the eco-conscious features of the residence.

AERIAL PHOTOGRAPHY IN THE HUDSON VALLEY

by Maxwell Alexander

Hudson Valley Homes and Estates really do have a lot of character, not to mention that the architecture, landscaping and nature setting is truly stunning. With the backdrop of the Hudson Valley, it is a prime location for aerial drone photography. With years of experience, it is safe to say that we work diligently to make sure that our clients get the result they want out of their aerial photography and this is especially the case if they are trying to sell or market their property. With breath-taking photographs and a friendly team who will work closely with you every single step of the way, you know that you can count on us to go that extra mile while also delivering remarkable and stylish photos that you never thought possible.

HARNESSING THE POWER & BEAUTY OF NATURE

We know that nature is truly a force to be reckoned with, but in the right situation, it can also provide you with the perfect setting for an inspiring photo shoot. It doesn't matter whether it is sunset, sunrise, in the middle of a heatwave or snowing like it's Christmas Day because we have the ability to use every situation to your advantage. This means that we capture photographs like you have never seen before and it also means that the end result won't be like every other real estate photography out there.

OUR TALENTED AND FRIENDLY TEAM

Led by Maxwell Alexander, World-Class Art Director and Photographer, our team knows exactly how to approach a luxury property with flawless execution. We take into account the style of the home, the surrounding greenery and more, before planning our angle of approach and camera view. This gives us the chance to capture your home in the best possible way while also giving us the chance to provide every single viewer (your potential buyer) with a unique and magical experience.

OUR DRONES AND PILOTS

When you come to us for all of your drone photography needs and requirements, you'll find that we have the latest professional equipment and only FAA-licensed drone pilots. Not only does this mean that we are able to deliver a better result than our competitors, but it also means that we have the experience you need to really stand out from the crowd.

OUR SPECTACULAR AERIAL REAL ESTATE PHOTOGRAPHY

Aerial Photography is one of the best ways to highlight your Real Estate Property including indoor and outdoor photo and video shots. We can cover landscape features and look and feel of the neighborhood, all of it is important to your potential buyers.

If you are interested in our team, how we can help you or even to see if there is anything that we can do for you then please do get in touch with us today. We would love to hear from you and we are very excited to work with you to get you the best result out of your aerial photography.

Review Our Aerial Photography Portfolio and Schedule Your Aerial Photo Shoot at DuncanAvenue.com

TO STAGE, OR NOT TO STAGE?

Learn More about this design project →
at duncanavenue.com/design

STAGED HOMES SELL 79% FASTER

STAGED HOMES SOLD IN 11 DAYS OR LESS
ON AVERAGE SPEND **73%** LESS TIME ON THE MARKET

COMPARED TO AVERAGE 90 DAYS ON THE MARKET

81% OF BUYERS
FIND THAT STAGING HELPS THEM BETTER **VISUALIZE** A PROPERTY AS THEIR **FUTURE HOME**

HIGHER SALES PRICES
STAGED HOMES SELL FOR **17% MORE** THAN NON-STAGED HOMES

BUYERS MOST OFTEN offer 1%-5% increase on the REAL VALUE OF A STAGED HOME

SELLERS SPEND LESS THAN 1% FOR STAGING SERVICES to get a 1000% RETURN ON INVESTMENT

HOME STAGING CAN BOOST PERCEIVED VALUE OF A HOME BY 20%

95% OF BUYER'S AGENTS SAY THAT HOME STAGING HAS A POSITIVE EFFECT ON THE HOME BUYER'S VIEW OF THE PROPERTY

3% YET LESS THAN 3% OF HOMES LISTED ON MLS ARE STAGED

DUNCAN AVENUE™
HUDSON VALLEY REAL ESTATE SERVICES

SCHEDULE YOUR CONSULTATION @
DUNCANAVENUE.COM

STATISTICS SOURCE:
NATIONAL ASSOCIATION OF REALTORS

HAVING YOUR HOME PROFESSIONALLY PHOTOGRAPHED?

by **Maxwell Alexander,** President, Chief Design Officer, Duncan Avenue Group

The real estate market in the Hudson Valley and around the Globe has been changing rapidly, and that has created some challenges for home sellers. It was not that long ago that searching for a home meant driving from New York City all the way to beautiful Hudson Valley neighborhoods, picking up flyers and sales packets and maybe stumbling upon on open house or two.

In the 21st century, home searches are more likely to start online while at lunch break in the office than in the family car. The ease of browsing real estate listings online is hard to beat, and potential buyers can scour dozens of listings in the time it would take to visit just one in person.

The shift to online home shopping has created both challenges and opportunities. If you understand how home buyers shop and what they are looking for, then you can make your listing stand out and rise above the rest. If you fail to put your home in its best light, would-be buyers could pass your home by as they do their online shopping.

Hiring a local Hudson Valley professional photographer is one of the best ways to make your home stand out. Duncan Avenue Real Estate Photography Studio is your premier professional photography provider in the Hudson Valley area including Orange, Rockland, Dutchess, Ulster, Putnam, Westchester, Greene, Rensselaer, Columbia, Saratoga and Albany Counties. We'll take care of making your online photographs stand out, but there are certain things you should do before the pro arrives. Here are the steps you should take while you wait for the photographer.

SECURE YOUR PETS

If you have a dog that is aggressive, territorial or just protective, be sure to secure the animal long before the photographer is scheduled to arrive. We love dogs, and in fact we've got two super hyper Jack Russell Terriers at home, however they could definitely get in a way of making your home look good in the pictures, especially if they are so cute that it's just way too distracting.

Even if your pets are not too aggressive, they could get in the way during the photo shoot. Placing your cats and dogs in the basement or garage is a courtesy you should extend to the professional who will be photographing your home.

START A FIRE

If your home has a fireplace, we would want to show it off. Be sure you have a roaring fire going in each of your fireplaces before the

[PHOTOGRAPHY STYLE]

HERE IS WHAT TO DO BEFORE THE PHOTOGRAPHER ARRIVES

photographer arrives.

A lit fireplace will not only make your home look inviting, but it also serves as proof that it's working correctly. A fireplace can be a big selling point, so do not sell yourself short.

| LIGHT SOME CANDLES

You can create a homey and inviting environment even if your home does not have a fireplace. Just pick your favorite candles, scatter them around the house and light them up when the photographer arrives.

A set of tapers on the table will create a romantic setting and make your finished photographs look great. A large pillar candle in the living room will create an inviting atmosphere and encourage browsers to take a look. Use your imagination, and ask your Hudson Valley Real Estate Photography Pro for other lighting ideas when he arrives.

| LIGHT IT UP

Speaking of lighting, turn all the lights on before the photographer's scheduled arrival. If any light bulbs are burned out, take the time to replace them. Set the dimmers to full power so that your home looks as bright and airy as possible.

You can let even more light in by rolling up the blinds and opening up the curtains. You want the space to be as bright and inviting as possible, and that brightness will come through in the finished photographs.

We will bring supplemental lighting with us to make sure all areas of your home look the best they can.

| CLEAR OUT THE DRIVEWAY

We would want shots of the driveway, so remove any cars, trucks or other vehicles before the scheduled photo shoot. Be sure to park them well down the street, keeping the road in front

of your home open as possible. Duncan Avenue Photography Studio is the only Real Estate Photography Studio that offers complementary FAA-licensed aerial/drone photography with every property or listing package.

Staging your home for open houses and private showings is important, but making your home look great in the listing photographs may be even more important. You can think of your listing photographs as a special kind of staging, one designed to draw the eyes of would-be buyers and get them to schedule a private appointment.

Make your appointment today at DuncanAvenue.com

MAXWELL ALEXANDER | HOME™

www.ingramcontent.com/pod-product-compliance
Lightning Source LLC
Chambersburg PA
CBHW051214220526
45473CB00003B/1033